eel on reef

eel on reef

Uche Nduka

BLACK GOAT
LOS ANGELES

BLACK GOAT is an independent poetry imprint of Akashic Books created and curated by award-winning Nigerian author Chris Abani. Black Goat is committed to publishing well-crafted poetry and will focus on experimental or thematically challenging work. The series aims to create a proportional representation of female, African, and other non-American poets. Series titles include:

Gomer's Song by Kwame Dawes
Auto Mechanic's Daughter by Karen Harryman

Published by Akashic Books
©2007 Uche Nduka

ISBN-13: 978-1-933354-37-8
Library of Congress Control Number: 2007926056
First printing

Black Goat
c/o Akashic Books
PO Box 1456
New York, NY 10009
info@akashicbooks.com
www.akashicbooks.com

For Ubanwa and Patricia

INTRODUCTION

by Kwame Dawes

Uche Nduka must know that his poems scrupulously defy the inclination toward singular meaning and clarity, and while one is tempted at times to ask the poet, "What do you mean here?" it does not take long for the reader to see that that would be an unwise choice. Apart from the likely untrustworthiness of the poet, there are other very good reasons to abandon such an approach. The truth is that in his absence, the poet leaves us with opportunities for such glorious indulgence, such imaginative excursions—the kind of exercises that make text-worshipping author killers elated. As readers we become writers when reading much of *eel on reef*. Why, for instance, should not the piece that opens with the lines *"on a slit and tit"* be about graffiti art or about the transgressions of outdoor sex? It would be a shame if Nduka came to tell us that the piece is loosely based on a Picasso painting and Yoruba myths of creation and regeneration.

> *on a slit and tit*
> *we make an arc.*
> > *a grape*
> > *heaves compassion*
> > > *on our thirst.*

> *we seek jerseyed*
> *phrases to hang*
> > *in a plaza.*

wash away my shadow
where a highway howls.
behind dimming lights
crab a leaf

     away
     from a tree. (23)

Nduka's poetry empowers the reader as poem slayer/maker. And yet, there is little doubt in the mind of the reader that we are engaged with a poet of beauty and tremendous musicality.

Reading Nduka's poetry is about granting yourself permission to enjoy each instant, each image, and to do so while beating back the instinct to construct linear meaning in the poems. Of course, Nduka will sometimes reward the linear reader—the reader who expects poems to be about something specific, to unfold along narrative lines, to deal directly with political and ideological themes. There are some poems that do so. After all, Nduka is acutely aware of his landscape and the politics of his world; as an African poet, he knows that while writing out of and sometimes against a tradition that seems bent on didacticism, he is also unable to ignore the rituals of lament and protest that one associates with that tradition. Such poems are exceptions—they are rare, and they only seem prosaic and accessible because they are planted among a dense thicket of inscrutable verse.

It is important then to try and find an approach to these poems. Halfway through the manuscript, I realized that what I was feeling was very familiar. Here is what I was feeling: I was stunned by the rich helpings of imagism—an intensely improvisational style that allowed juxtapositions, counterpoint, repetition, and surprise to be the rigid task masters of the poems. I was also impressed by the extensive vocabulary, the literary instinct that understood how to carefully avoid the familiar (one can't avoid the familiar without being familiar with the familiar). Yet, I also felt a certain unease and disquiet. I was not comfortable with not understanding the poems—not understanding everything in the poems. This unsettled me. On the one hand, I felt as if the poet was working too hard to confuse me and I resented that. And on the other, I feared that this was hardly what the poet was doing—that, in fact, the poet was simply so brilliant that my poor brain could not keep up with him. I found myself working hard to find an anchor, a way to engage the work. It was hard because I kept being distracted by the beauty of the language, the shock of the images, and the deft slippage of meaning all over the place. I had been there before. The last poet to do that to me was Christopher Okigbo when I first read him. But Okigbo gave me more—he gave me Eliot-like footnotes and assured me that somehow, if I kept at it, I would arrive at the Holy Grail of meaning. Yet he taught me that I was better off applying a Zenlike act of release in reading his poems if I wanted to truly enjoy them.

Tellingly, Nduka's poetry led me in the same direction. I stopped thinking too hard and I simply read, sometimes out loud, relishing the playfulness, the punning, the idiomatic expressions, the striking metaphors, and the studied brevity of form. Nduka can be delicious when taken out of context; the reason is simple—he is wont to be taken out of context because he is clearly not interested in context and all its elements. He avoids titles all together. He avoids sections. He eschews epigraphs. He resists easy allusions. He backs away from narrative for as long as he is able. Consequently, it is possible to randomly select a series of brilliant images from the work, that on their own are beautifully evocative:

> *a corn husk in a dollhouse.* (30)
> *nursemaid vaccinating filth?* (29)
> *upon your summering affection* (74)
> *wealth tempers all truncative interventions.* (106)
> *a heart that rains paints / on blades* (31)

Taken in tiny morsels like this, the poems reward slow contemplation and consideration. Their riddles are usually dense enough to satisfy further scrutiny. Even when we are left nonplused by the images, there is something satisfying about the effort to make sense of the lines that we encounter.

Yet, this collection is one that we read through quickly. Part of the reason is the absence of markers—without titles, we have the sense that we are reading an extended diatribe, and the language has a simplicity and an odd and deceptive familiarity. These abstractions are three dimensional and so have a "realness" to them. The allusive possibilities of the poems are stunningly encyclopedic, but since we do not take advantage of the process of reflection and meditation, we easily rush over images, quickly arriving at the next while still harboring an anxiety that we have not done justice to the last.

One of Nduka's earlier poems in the sequence offers a fitting metaphor for the entire collection.

> *a season trembles.*
> *the sentience of a season*
> *quivers inside water . . .*
>
> *a shining turtle plays*
> *in your splashing vista.*
> *i wish i could*
> *estrange your starfish*
> *from a pebble.* (21)

The organizing metaphor for these poems is the underwater world where meaning is obscured by the physical mutability of water—the illusionary play of light in such depth, the disorientation caused by airlessness, and the reminder that there is much we don't know about the depths. Here is a metaphor then for poems intent on shattering linearity and semantic order. The effect is a studied surrealism. Nduka's formal practice is carefully structured around the use of the riddle or a metaphor that may or may not lead to illumination. But illumination is a peculiar thing. Often we seek out tangible meaning—a kind of direct correlation between metaphor and meaning. Nduka is not constrained by such limitations of illumination. The surprise of a successfully shaped juxtaposition of sound and word is revelation enough for him; and the rhetorical challenge is to do that in each poem.

In a poem that begins, "*how can i say in words / things i didn't*

/ *understand through words?*" (87) Nduka offers an insight into how he rationalizes what may appear to be poetry intent on puzzling. The question is a sharply realized one because it offers the reader the idea that Nduka regards what he is doing as a poet using words as a wholly inadequate response to the idea, to the image that has haunted him. For him, words will never do justice to the idea that has formed in his head. Nduka in this poem asks a series of seemingly unanswerable questions, but the very process of questioning is essential to his project:

> *how serious can i*
> *take the suggestion of*
> *this river searching for an ocean?*
>
> *how involved are twisting*
> *suckers in boyism in girlism?*
> *who sponsored water*
> *in the ventures of my land?*
>
> *on behalf of whom*
> *do stars dissect the night?*
> *who surrendered to water*
> *a portion of a salt hill?* (87)

By the time we come to the end of the poem, we know that there will be no answers. Each question can be seen as monumental. In the final stanza the scope of the inquiry is epic—this is a question about divinities that may or may not shape our ends. The last question is classic Ndukaism for its weighty intelligence—a mask that suggests that there is something profound about the line. And even as we search out the allusions (Lot's wife comes to mind), we wonder whether we are going too far. We are also not sure whether we should allow ourselves to take some solace in the idea that the poet is simply questioning how the sea became salty. Either way, we are left with questions that are decidedly impossible to answer. And it is in this that we find the slippage of meaning that is so important to Nduka.

Yet, as I have said, the thing that manages to relieve frustration is Nduka's sensuality. In line after line, we find an erotic quality—a fascination with bodies, with sexuality, with clothing, with tastes and smells. His poetry is rich with sensory triggers and playful references to sex:

> *centralize my prayers*
> *certify my wankings*
>
> *fumigate cultivate*
> *the gardens of my body . . .*
>
> *my attempts to come ashore*
> *upon your summering affection* (74)

In an earlier poem, Nkuda offers outrageous juxtapositions of the sacred and the sensual:

> *do they need a pilgrimage*
> *to lhasa, lourdes, mecca?*

eggnog and commode
serve up peptonic chatter
a disquisition on
                wearers of slutskirts
                        minus leggings

or the fable of cotton
black lace, black basque
black tie, black thong

                the breathing stalk
                in between a fleshy cleavage. (22)

A curious thing happens when Nduka produces poems that
appear to have a political bent — one that would not be satisfied
with enigma. The reader has been so prepared by the absurdist
sensibilities in the work that when he presents the grotesquerie
and absurdist violence of "real" human experience and tragedy,
one senses nothing whimsical. Indeed, the surrealism that
emerges is a commentary on the violence and the horrible facts
behind the poem. The subtext is that what has become a tragic
reality for many Africans can only be articulated through the
language of the absurd:

        in hospital,
        tunnel
        forest, road

below bridges
whose faces are
made up with chalk

i think of
furtive massacres
amputated legs
swollen necks

needless subtractions
senseless intrusions

clotted routes
charred swallows

falling
from
silence
to
silence. (43)

At the end of the day, I find that Nduka's poems have grown on me. They are the kinds of poems that would probably please the Imagists during their heady, idealistic years—poems that are comfortable with the centrality of image. And all the descendants of the Imagists would find Nduka's dogged desire to confound and to thus stretch the function of the poem at once alarming and affirming. I find myself wanting to steal Nduka's lines in the way that I find myself stealing images when I walk through a gallery of contemporary paintings. I am also struck by how much I do not care if I don't understand the images before me — I am just entranced with the intuitive engagement that I have with the poems the more that I read them.

It must be said that in Nduka we have an African writer who is willing to defy the sometimes intense pressure to assume the role of griot — a kind of community poet who must write proverb-filled epics rooted in the culture. However, this poet is driven by the same impulses as others before him — the quest for music in language; a quest that in the best of times results in something beautiful and strangely new:

> *the music in a bird*
> *is what you've*
> *broken into two.*
>
> *slideaway facedown.*
> *your breath is still*
> *besotted with*
>
> *the eel on a reef.*
> *where you've beached*
> *stars hang on scales*
> *of water.* (140)

eel on reef

a season trembles.
the sentience of a season
quivers inside water.
the sun slaps a wall.
where is your face?
tuck your hair
into a band.
where is your face?
pat back your hair
let me see your face.
a shining turtle plays
in your splashing vista.
i wish i could
estrange your starfish
from a pebble.

hollyhocks and earwigs:
do they need repairs?
do they need judges?
do they need a pilgrimage
to lhasa, lourdes, mecca?

eggnog and commode
serve up peptonic chatter
a disquisition on
      wearers of slutskirts
         minus leggings

or the fable of cotton
black lace, black basque
black tie, black thong

      the breathing stalk
      in between a fleshy cleavage.

on a slit and tit
we make an arc.
     a grape
     heaves compassion
          on our thirst.

we seek jerseyed
phrases to hang
     in a plaza.

wash away my shadow
where a highway howls.
behind dimming lights
crab a leaf
        away
        from a tree.

street one. here.
first fire. there.
skate to reggae's gate.
nothing matters to you
but the handshake of wheat.
not unguents.
                not pestles.
                    not toys.
a soundslinger
calls out to dogs.
            rascality blinks
                between
                    the feet
                      of his answerers.

skylight,
  silverlight
    and a beagle.
the alley hasn't hurt my words.
  a lion in a ledge
    hounds a skipper.

to night-trippers
    of a crooked nation
there are still oaths to be sung.

what you call a sprightly stroll
i call a barbituric swagger.

abandon your wristwatch now.
forget computed pantheons.
look at a mismatch.

                laces gone hazy.

simulacra.

               furrowed choir.

a rumble in a bramble.

into the lament of a gong
            a dreambird has wandered.

a primping flyrod
halts your rising frown.
you don't have to let up
on your aces or be
elegantly dummied—you
don't have to let your
silence disarm a hoesong.

and the consolation of displeasure?

drums swallow rattles.
potholes eat boots.
yet a greenscreener
      needs a snowplow.
      a water diviner
      needs a donkey's jaw.
      a remote patrol
      needs a tuba's tongue.

and the global tribesman?

they hoot at tips of fire,
    idiocy draped
             round their guns.
   in their stripes
            rodents roam.
     scurvy bites into their kinship.
the coal marks on their lips
          mock a stripper
whose friend is left
        with an empty cup
   in a flashbox.

a painted beard of red
becomes a painted beard of blue
when the moon dawdles
around in the afternoon.
when 4 becomes 8
and 2 becomes 6.

does kerosene ever sleepwalk
as it moves within a wick?

in our house there are seven missing doors.

and where is the village
nursemaid vaccinating filth?

in our town there is a lake between our dreams.

our rivers are capped.

spice the night
behind a light —
there is a rectangle
in an octagon.
an octagon in a hexagon.
a corn husk in a dollhouse.
throw your multitasking mantle
to keepers of a cross-dressing date.
wave your headstick.
get caught in midnet.
overfishing
is the job of a beachbody.

which brings us
          to the fag-end of
a tenure in a milk bar

and swingtets in corpuscles
                    isles in nerves

with their creepy-crawlies,
                    tiger lilies

that recall the treason
               of amniotic fluid

a heart that rains paints
               on blades,

          a blizzard of feathers.

                addresses.
there are addresses in trees
where rains go to die.
tents.

there are spousal tents
    where halo-seekers
    wash their toes
    and house their grudges.

you're moaning again.
           no.
you're moaning again.
no. i'm like a cat. i'm
purring. i'm happy.

sandblasters, slanghewers
in inns and dives,
the laxatives of lampposts
at night in lanes:
agonies marched
to and fro over them.
       errors of raillery
         spring from
           olives grazing
            on smiles
              of nodding sojourners.

your father was
a seaman who could
not disown the bells
of the waves.

a liquid sessioneer, he bawled:
give me some mammaries!
where is your stepladder?
where is your screwdriver?

his gigs were interactive.

he mined your line
for age and rust
and made you wobble and
sink in the dust.

his nuggets, frameable.

does touching make
the flesh row
a boat
of song?

       here
           the noon
           is talking backwards.

a fishing sun
    blesses the last
        trek of nouns.

  every crevice
    of a tune
        surrenders
           to the flesh.

a story burns.
    a window turns.
        in the peninsula.

the wagon carver
    strides backward.
the saddle carver
    sprints forward.

trying to fly a kite
the rain scratches
the mind of a tree.

those are not the bellies
of pumpkins;
those are the narcotics
of their divergencies.

at the great sun-meeting
where are the recalled ambassadors?
at the diplomatic castle
where are the uncloaked spies?
            help! help!
      where are the mushrooms?

and the alternation of horrors
as in the constant search
of blueness in grayness
rain in smoke
moonsand in flamestone?

between sulking porches
moondreamers knead mooneggs.

a masseuse bestowed
a gamekeeper upon
your gas pipes

your gas pipes
buttressed the savage
laughter of a swishing mantilla

a swishing mantilla
beckoned kleptomaniacs
giantesses, auctioneers

knit a quilt with
horsehoof and batwing
for naked sopranos to lie on

may the flute remember
    bonehills, red glares
    bare barns,
                oscillatory oaths

                the campaigning needle
                after a tonguebath

did they not accuse him
of sinfully wearing
                velvet trousers?

                swisshh!

but did he piss on the moon?
did he boil the breeders
            of hydrogen bombs?

                was he lefting?
                was he righting?

                honeycup!

the curves of recessional
cycles;
the dotted segments, the
vertices foretold of stuttering
minds;

and us making ducks drunk
by offering them pieces
of bread dipped in vodka
beside the lake;

the stampede
as they search for foxprints —
       squaak! squaaakk!
squaaaakkk!

boots and bulbs
swaying in the treetops;
moon boats sliding across
planet lights etc.

from attic
    to caboose

a chattering shadow
    outdances

a plowhorse
   and catfish.

chants
    graze in
    our canefields.

to us,
   all words
    are destinies.

black legs, brown hairs
and
under them,
grandpa's victrola.

night is a pal. (plainly)
night is a game
inside a clock. (counterfeitedly)

outside where
        a weeder smoothens
the soil
    of a cassava ridge

the night is a neighbor
    that looks on each
time maroko is
        hurled to nocturnal gallows.

brown hairs, black legs
and
under them,
bootprints bootprints.

in hospital,
tunnel
forest, road

below bridges
whose faces are
made up with chalk

i think of
furtive massacres
amputated legs
swollen necks

needless subtractions
senseless intrusions

clotted routes
charred swallows

falling
 from
silence
 to
silence.

who's going to plough
the fetal furrow?

mustn't always take
what i find—

slick deputizing
paragraphing maestro

fabric, waxwork
stars in a quarry

or the latest pause
on the road

for munchkins waving
bratpop

solipsis.

    the cousinly gray
        in a goatee.

                equipoise.

your acoustic no
    to the demolition of

the grace of a child
    in san diego.

    the raping of a son
        by the mother.

    the raping of a daughter
        by the father.

ratdogs. rusted roots.

corroded by fate in death
you still do not hold
back your steps.

the wide street you walk
        is a wide skirt.
the screamer in your scream.

corroded by fate in death
you still tweak
the noisefest
of an open mic.

timpani, dobro, seastone.

a rushing of fibers and fragrance
your legs crossed, uncrossed
la singla!

hills mingling with veins
your legs slanting, grinding
                    on floorboard.

la singla!
the fire of your feet

the art of your fire
la singla!

your clatter your patter
a masquerade in trance

as your life sways
around hems, ribbons

la singla!

in the midtown
     of your midriff
is a pointing finger

you're salsa
     merengue
guaracha, bolero

     spearminting
          cuntdrunk

     landstitching
          a rain like a footwear—

your rising penis
     is the rising sun

noon show me
the homebrush
show me the
wordshop noon

noon show me
the insteps of the
rough and the sweet
how they lacerate a stoic

show me the
purgatorial meeting
of two winds noon
their upended agenda

noon show me
the red-eyed mouse
in a cage
show me the
nude with red sandals noon

if you don't want me
maybe you'll want
the four-armed candelabra
        you'll want
fishnets and bone necklaces

if you don't need me
maybe you'll need
the axeman the waterman
        you'll need
the mutations of car crash
                and coitus

to scratch your blisters
to scratch your kind

a mastiff sniffing
  a wire fence

notices a gloved restaurant
  a sweating volkswagen

where teasing cinnamon
  and lemonade

  are not forbidden

our hands laden
  with herbs

our legs ringed
  by nights

nights crazed by yams

arousers
      uppers

gestural hesitancies
of lust
in
tandem;
    spice
    of baby bulge
  and bump
      between us;

birds in our boat
heads on grasses
dust of innocence
heeling in
heeling out

sunsets shuttle through
gauzes and bins
on their way home on their
way home

earthrise sells alibis
wakes up to oilhill
compost, moneymountain

sunsets can't lie
to sunsets nor to
the brilliant blood
of an aged eggshaker

you burn maps
stain your sex
mutilate your shoebox

          hurl back
an oathtime to my ken
          hurl back
a wirewall, a soundcard, odometers

i shoot snooker
          on a flab-busting
stint in a poolhall

or am i otherwhere
          in the middle
of quixotic switches?

i'm movable slideable
          like knifemarks
on biceps that bulbs
                    missee

wacky is he sung
by the linden trees of berlin

do i mistake the scene
for the mudland irokos of agbor?

sniffy is he stretched
to the fate of floating gossamer

saying to be turbanned
is not to be eased into a caul

larky is the nutcracker in a
henhouse flowing from flaw to flaw

the bite of bile widens the
jazz of his voracious nights

chibuzo oguekwe,
prepare the cassava.
stir the bitterleaf sauce.

nobody crosses the knees
of streams anymore
or waits for us after
school, the way they did
when we were mornings.

no one's thread flares
to patch the torn seats
of our trousers. nowadays
nobody bares the provincial
scrawls on blackboards.

kid! don't you recognize
yourself? here, take
these bracelets, my child,
before the matrist synod
turns ontological.

seaspray, ah!

>	your rope begins to quiver
in your hand.
it smells of the sartorial
hanging of a weakling.

ennui flattens the acrobat.
omniscience grafts itself
to his fateful wilding.

and the weather? isn't it
there to be ignored
by you?

you bypass the rosewater
on the seacoast as well.
you refuse a sonata
and opt for a waltz.

>	ah, seaspray!

all around hailstones
thump mudwalls

i indulge myself
in enamelled idylls

lovely are the farms
beyond a shaded pigsty

not hounded nor cornered
azuka rolls me round

verandas and rooms
in a pram with wooden wheels

not by my father nor by my mother
but by my grannies and nannies and aunties

was i reared.
was i rustled to life.

wahoo this seismic keg
unplug this room
        from the socket of the earth

into your closed eyes
            let chlorine
                    shine

into stalactites
                into sausage rolls

    let serenatas roll

                be regal again

remove the sables
            from the shoulders
    of the gunner on the run

                from brayful larynxes
                rheumatic motorics.

fuck all the frescoed fuck-ups.

segueing into a chanting
duel and a tweezing trip
a guffawer braids
a trail to a houser.

it's triangular—
the percussive festivity
of a solar pilgrim
on a barstool.

as the houser
as the guffawer
as the jazzer
you air out chalkdust.

the gourd
the mudcrutch
belong to your backpack
        to your hitchhiking

not to melons dressed
                in nylons
not to toygins not to
                dollgins.

when shall your wounds
welcome their scabs?

daily your kingdom squeaks
and leaps to the starlight

it wants all of you
you of all and the music

of the pastures of midnoon
a little boy's kaleidoscopticon

you are the one the music
has chosen and whom strings call

twilight moans behind you
all you are you are all

it is the boy in black talking
how civil is the civil war?

sadly sings the moonlit
glass under a thatch.

a hooded jewess
drifts in escalators of light.

flatirons are addicted
to her presence.
porcelains are
addicted to her presence.

she is the fence.
she is the vine.
she is standing.
she is bending.

a confessor crosses her tracks.

do it if you can—
number the pieces
of my crashed heart.

label their smoke plumes.

the red arch of
a hill wears my flesh.
my crag's in rags.
my burlesque's panned.

read the virulent words.

i'm solitude rowing
through neons patterned
after the life
of a night. a dog's bark

rushes the fingers
of a keyboardist, not pleading
not begging, behind

an outspread umbrella.

a mountain splits.
footsteps measure the broken earth.
rocks die.

not in abeyance is the anguish
of the andean woman
of the mountain.

she makes roads.
roads make her.
she returns to water
where waterwheels speak.

are you reminded, sister
of the lemon grove
of your ravaged heights?

and a voice to burn with arrives
    in tripled frenzy
    in cyclic precision

and his groin-gazing
    the whiff of his heel
and his turbo-thrust

where every imp is a patriot
      every thug a savior
      every screamer an apostle
      every nosepicker a prophet
      every crook a statesman.

at a banquet urbanites
shame the instinctual
league of bipeds.
ten-steppers
terrorize antimacassars.
a nodal curve ascends
to bellies forbidden
to stand forbidden to seat.

driven, raw fire dogs
the contours of a log.
a herdgirl's eternity gestures
from astral larva.
her laughter is flameshine
on semantic tentacles.
her penumbra
renews the breeze's profile,
the cliff-banger,
a migrating parchment.

my edges are spidering.
sort of.
shredding my connection
to a tanned belief.
to a yellow house.

i promise skits to players.
i juke. i saw off thorns.
i face a bank. a warlock.
a tank. i make time spit.
toss wrinkles off my flank.

valor isn't a lap dance.
i scrawl. i slam. i sprawl.
i'm fragile. that is.
i growl. i mumble. i squiggle.
my lines are birds flying
inside a page full of darts.

a noontimer stands, aims straight
and kicks the gathering shit
with the argot of shit
pray pray for him

the prodigy's tongue is
for grilling and the iced shit
borne in gales of gray
is for drowning

let's read then the thesis
of a buffoon and proclaim
the apocrypha that is
making our ears salivate

go ahead and die
you horde of doom,
framegrabber brasstender!
the earth starts whelping one afternoon in june.

the empty cities go singing
their empty songs.
thief thief don't come here.
walk on, menacer.
barbarous harvester.
don't come here to
feign the miracle of talismans.
keep away your soothsaying—
your pretext for mental thieving
for letting loose your
grenades on virile triangles.
joy-shunning, blood-drinking
you stab stab stab
horses for neighing
wrens for singing
land-thief land-thief
keep your alchemical gift to yourself.

concretely dead is the putrescent
behemoth in a radiant orchard.
for man begins where
a metropolis ends. so let's rise
to the orphic door. let's
leave the falling leaves of
the falling shadow. when gardens
grow bloody and courtyards
become macabre let's
seek the lustrous arms of
sainted whores. may priestesses
meet priests. may flagellants
turn hedonists when on
their chests fall the eyes of blame.

wisebath, winefroth, coconuts
were your offerings to ulasi.
now you bring
chokebone and shuttlecock
                    only.

who stumbles in the depot
of my colored numbers?
                    you ride
your swindle beyond
                    the whistling
arse of a river.
                    beyond the
machined heart of a timber near it.
your sign bites my navel.

it makes me shiver.

a few repairs are called for
    in the valley
so the resident river protests
    as it should

and above the valley, trousered,
you do not mistake
the voice of the river
for that of the vulture.

tasting blood, spraying cant
water's matriarchy palms
knifed selves, incisions, poisons.
shadows nose through
your encounters, your treacheries

though you are still stoned on music.

zapped is our depressive vibe
in a silent kiosk.
your bra clutches my tie.
it's an acidic hold.

you've been everything
but a reveller
inside a grassy whorl.
everything but a night
chewing fur.

the mellow siren of a moonspell
illuminates our truce
with fiddling dildos.

centralize my prayers
certify my wankings

fumigate cultivate
the gardens of my body

my interrogational
abysses and crossings

my attempts to come ashore
upon your summering affection

leaven with delight
my fisherfolk my naturalists

the vagaries of faith
on the edge of days

absolve needy eyes
from fractal entrapments.

in convalescence we return
to our dualities and contraries.

we connive in the mauling of crickets.
see their obituarists.

keep a rein on all icons
of graffiti, write the obituarists.

avoid bards that wear red
and slay their mission,
             advise the obituarists.

while riddles steam our depths
mimers boast they will
bomb off the dawn,
             report the obituarists.

a reflexive reference to towerblocks
recalls to us the weavings
of probing pamphlets.
you steer clear of a broadcaster's
red graphs and aural etchings
of ancestresses unfathomed,
acrimonies in parenthesis.
for you aren't afraid
of owners of bronzed wrists,
tonal aviations,
night coughs that sound
from clay-tips to clay-kilns.

i broach again the desecration
of a collegian's quest.

i am the observer and the observed.

i am among the findings
in holy wells and redemptorist mountains.

get on your bike—fast—fast
before a flood hits your head.

sayeth the posters:
are you looking for paid unemployment
stop making sense
you are out of print
a cigar cannot walk alone in the rain
thanks for smoking

run—run—take a front seat
again on your bulky backside.

a window's mouth opens
out to the visitation
of a waking saluting planet.

dragging along a scrap of bread
a mouse moves under a carved
mask to salivate, eat, meditate.

the flavor of escape decreases.

isn't it atrocious
bursting your pimples
in front of a streetmirror?

darkness takes over
darker than dark
closer than close.

serpentine storms
coil round ears of rain.
where are your shoes?
where is your belt?

monologues of breakers
do more than suggest your
sounds and you
as i surf in you.

wearing beards and beads our hours
do headstands and push-ups.
a punkette with ankle bracelet
burnishes our focal dalliance.
will she liberate our genealogical charts too?
        the grove of her flesh
situates waterfalls necking with hills.

stunners breathe on fingers
on apostolic missions of pleasure.
they breathe on. they breathe on.

we are wilding.
       going to lick
       ourselves into distress.

anyhow.

she is a shout.
      her story bleeds.
you're her raspy double.
      but trees love you.

sing to my wounds.
sing to my burns.

"tomorrow never starts
unless you let today begin."
it isn't easy being green.

revive your visions.
      revive your ravines.
bend to a starlight.

what has taken from
a woman the milt
with which she seeks beauty?

a powdered dawn?
a dusk's declension?
gravelled sophistry?

where stems die
her decapitations teeter
between surreal osculations.

the blacker the eyes,
the skimpier the dress,
the better her table-hopping gets.

will you leap from an elevator,
lie on a long carpeted corridor,
spread your hands as if on a cross and say
—sometimes i am jesus christ—?
                        will you race out again from
a bathroom
your eyes addled with fright
to complain your parents
whom you claimed were inside
tried to dispatch you from
life through strangulation?
or point to corners of our room
where electronic listening devices
were presumably placed by our enemies?
or vanish from my side on a sunday morning
with your tattered green bag
while i snore and trip and snore?

already you simply are.
      i'm still being extended
                by you.

you watch television.
a kitestring watches you.
lower than your necklines
repetitive hungers shudder
           among textiles.

are you watching a waterplay,
waterart, or floatable flame?

in a blooming future
a host shall be a guest in disguise.
a greeter shall greet herself.
visitors shall visit themselves.

disobey your archetypes
when a totem rises.
offer mercury to earthhouses.
perfect the milkmusic
of the underjaw.

even voidoids are tired
of travels in liquid.
tired of shellseekers,
piggy-backed swimmers;

marshy pools in a wood.

are we only to have
flowers and fruits
talk to us
at table,
hug us
with stalks,
chasten us
with
seeds where snowflakes
veil our blemishes?

water splashes through itself
and into its own door.
we dive into it
and emerge on the other side
of a glistening tabernacle.
a *unio mystica*?

we fall into ourselves.
we fall like rainsnakes and rain,
droplets on bellies and
details of sailing.
without our knowing,
we are water's burden.
fugitives from
the hotchpotch of highrise blocks.

how can i say in words
things i didn't
understand through words?

how serious can i
take the suggestions of
this river searching for an ocean?

how involved are twisting
suckers in boyism in girlism?
who sponsored water
in the ventures of my land?

on behalf of whom
do stars dissect the night?
who surrendered to water
a portion of a salt hill?

you danced slaveships into you.
rejoiced at bloated bodies.
chained hands and feet
flattered your waves.
you betrayed your algae
your conches your anemones.

i'm a victim of your speech
yet i like to hear you speak.
perishable is sleep perishable is sleep
yet i like to fall asleep beside you.

water knocks on
the gate of your tongue.
you leave a toytown.

i don't know if it was
the lightning that glittered on
your bed that cracked your bed.

there where you wish to be
      —beyond dykes—
the night speaks the patois of roots.

purple is the lighthouse
from which you stare and spit
at throngs fluttering
to hem you in and throw you down
where gravities shake.

a landscape's lexicon lapses
in your sullen expression.
(don't turn around)

humus greets you
flint greets you
coal takes apart
            your echoing leafage.

encircled, advanced upon, beaked,
knowledge radiates your artery.
music ignites your fountain.
                  i see you thickening.

i see you rustling.
unsullied by thoughts
by gestures by silence,
            plateaus invent your creed.

images don't talk anymore
in the sands of your underslope.
a festival starts in your lips in
your knees lighted by your hair's glare.

i can't hide the heat of my heart
in a shadowdale. in a tunneltrance.
or in scrubbing of slippery floors
or washing of pillowcases.

you may be the changeling
i'm looking for.
the earthling i'm looking for.
                for now, at least,
you're not this garlic
whose shirt i'm removing.

and i can't hide
in those songs
that have strayed
in the rooms
of a guitar.

moonmad
stonemad
i shall
pass like
                night.

a sword's red track
a bullet's stained blade
the balled flame of a volcano's
                        tantrum

does not care if i am
or if i am not the dreamer
                i dream of.

asters and pansies:
they can be streets,
                they can be vales.

for they also kill and rape and torture:
            those posted to enforce peace
                        on your shore.

they walk on bones,
                transact with blood —
bug, rove, piss.

i do not fold the sky,
                i widen it.

salamanders collide in
your bedding. adobes
blend with sharkskin.
                    you sharpen
your taste for villainy.
you enlarge
                    your snare.
                    what
you're thundering to stir
                    are all of me.

but a sunflower covers
                    your sex.

i slant between pomp and doom.
mourning maniacs.
                    gyrating
where masculinities are impaled,
                    horsebreaking.

between us, an echo grows.

with your purse your satin
you stream to cobalt waters.
you're a trapper.
you squint through a drizzle,
walk through a parade
to this place where you
work up a cold udder
to a sweaty twang.
also you're a tapper
with reddish hair stamping
on the jaws of jadeites.

to the end
the sailors we see
know survival is navigable.
why care about
reading ribs that earn their lights?
our love's loaded
with jasmine and dung like all loves.

an alarm stabbed my sleep.
a berserker hid my body.
i woke on your mandala
and no waking was ever
so ascendant and provident.

ropethrower, concretepourer:
did you feel the drowsing air?

the night was walking
        the night was winding.

her come-hither lips said
        dip your paddle
                dip your paddle.

sunwavers and tinted fishes clash.
                are you watching?
                are you raising
                a countertenor?

as suns converge
as jungle-jumping starts
as requiems gather

                they toss flowers
                at your passing hearse
                accused by their guilt.

and return to
the trap-laden water,
to the squeezed metal
the nocturnal tunnel
that newly made
you an ancestress.

indifferently, you drummed
inside the womb that was
            your first earth.

now we take turns
eyeing the plates, the shelves
            the curtains
                    inside a room.

outside, people sit under
the friendly shadows
            that trees make.

clouds begin their flagwaving.
haven't our lives just begun?
winds begin to preach.
do you hear the sermons
                    of the winds?

inwards to the saltwater
tides haunt you. you chafe!
you hasten into the flesh
of a birth in september.
how brief your gestation!
how wide the unclaimed
assemblage of tokens!
                    but you've
chosen chronologies,
                      fugues, preludes.
out from the mud and blood
of a term's cloister
you declare yourself
a partisan of trees, milk, melodies.
shorn of ponchos you come
to propitiate heights,
avert curses, douse tantrums.

to rhetoricize the fervor
of seaflowers
is plain dismemberment.
on the waterline
hills await their crucifixions.
deeper and deeper
through breaking glass
grains break. a siege approaches.
who brought the steerage passage
                    to the concavity
and convexity of your wickerwork?
which people are
they meant to serve,
your answers
that end in bayonet points?

every week in the pigsticking year
someone wakes the verities
of your machine. why? don't
answer. don't possess a heart,
be the heart itself, the heart itself.
turn tightly to biddable alembics.
seek askers who tackle tyrannicides.
                    (not innocuously.)
nwugo aneke
                nwugo aneke

flow back to me
        swim back to me

into a robin's nest
            i ask you to venture again.

as loveliness appropriates
an afternoon
a ripe text
refreshes
our
finitude.
how
does
silence break us?
how
does
errancy knead us?
the
blade
of your gaze
exchanges
an oath
with a plowlander.
what is downward
            is the encounter.
what is upward
            is the encounter.

boat me around gently.
whoever i'm with
i'm seeing only you.

diplomacy has wounded us.
pierced us. smashed us.
is there something
in the turning
of this river's head
that will mend our dislocations?

your eagle drives my ego.
there is ice in your thighs.

take the buoys of light
for your thighpaths whose
eyes

night has darkened.

in white robe
far from water
in white headdress
far from water
romance reins him in.
the bedouin, i assure you,
does not love his gun
more than his woman.
he has no tree
on which to carve hearts and arrows
but a wall. a wall. a wall.
yet stones and sands
do not restrain
the words of his lovetalk in sinai.
in sinai. in sinai.

long have you searched
the crests of waves
for routes of freedom.
in the tussle between
a grin and a din,
which is going to win?
have you forgotten him
who plays king
where grasses grow long?
he moistens pogroms
that curve, earth that
floods. his parables bleed.
his webs stiffen. bitterness
veins into striations of his
search, of his noise, of his role.

within your cylinder
is lingam is yoni;
    scarab sitting
        on a lotus.

i've never heard you
apologize for cropping
the brains of green crabs

or for being a gunning sea
a spalling medium
a panopticon.

elsewhere, your raw
expressions compromise
the judgments of oars.

no matter. my trope knows
whereof it speaks.
our voices are appurtenances
splashed beyond gourds
to fructify. no ray is
laughable to a hole in a kernel.
your protectorate entraps
our cities, our gods,
our children, our goddesses.

it does seem, still, that no
one can blotch out our credences.
wealth tempers all truncative interventions.

but you wouldn't wish it
to be so. you invite
familiarity with intrepid paupers.
to daybreak rowers
you refuse explanations.
thus your deed has braided
into my hair an aquamarine beret.
i launch steps against your desire.
my yard has great need for fences.

exact and exacting
are pastures of water.
unhip.
uncool.
then hip, then cool.
you
stride,
hurling chains
through
      fish tanks.

      at water's
door you stop.
then mount reefs.
slide under foam.
track carcasses.
         you survey
your mind,
alternating between
the conversational encroachment
of loss and belief.

take back thoughts.
bark at limbs clinging
to graffiti in water.
take back pity.
create a street of rafts.
take off your earrings.
dive.

a garrulous ferry
quakes across a wharf.
a barge
     delves into tired mud.

dive where liners don't
          gauge their speed!
dive into water's lascivious
            disarray!
dive beneath brown water's
          knees!

     adulthood roils—
not controlled—not granulated—
   not excused—

       in all directions.

they push out the boater
for heavy thinking
     and
       heavy dreaming.

       mutter murder.

mutter murder.

    like a girdle is
      the mustache around
          his nipple
      the barnacle around
          his name

    bargains spearing into
         his emergencies,
breathlines, existentialist quotas
        abomunist newscast.

regarding placement,
the pebble before him
is not hypertensive —

the rocks steadying him
         are not syntactic —

how can he plug
his torment
into phrasal
nomenclature?

water laps against his fatigue.

firebirds
         eye
waterseeds.

regarding casting —

who is that singing
              of unctuous genuflections?

who is the stoker
              coding the march of troops

across blue veins?

up comes the dawn,
              the dawn of their cruise,

waving, flying.

up comes the dawn,
              the dawn of their abyss,

smoldering, squirming.

vessels ratify their silhouettes.
              ratify their routes.

routes at stake.

frontiers of tragedy.

websiting, hitchhiking, freighthopping

crumbling under

verbalists,

circus tumblers,

ventriloquists,

jokers,

under the catafalque of bridges
under the garlanded streams
under the frenzied rivers
under the hounded seas.

we nod to one another
spiral through hedges
welcomes
arrivals
goodbyes
departures
dazed by the devotion
of surfboards and beachcombers.

sepulchral ruin that i hug
ruin that i flee from
leaving your ant-columns
leaving your marshlands

spin me with pizzazz
perfume me with thyme
kindle my minuet—

clammers
netters
breakers.

rocky outcroppings
shoulder to shoulder
with rockhounds—

dripping florists
        whitewashing frost—

their songs lean on a salmon,
unsmiling, half-cracking
the balconies of waves,
fixing crabs in their places,
entering the ruins of sunk
ships

higher and lower
        higher and lower

            water slapping water
            log probing leaf
            feet on shed dress
            set loose by horizon
            no path no path no path
                    to ascend.

your knee your knee
      there in the railing

(minus cotton fabric)

      threads itself to

the hazard of
      a trawler subjected

to landlessness.

your hand your hand
      there on nettle

(minus lotion)

      the seaspray scatters

sadness
      over it.

your mouth your mouth
      grasps varnishing soundings

(minus tongue)

where moorings fail

and a gull's wings revolve

in a current.

through wombholes you see.
through spasms.
     legitimize
          the early
judgments

     of ruralities;

pooldance
seadance
streamdance.

     dislocate your routine.
     sleep off your dirt.

in dreamsex
     you can patent

     your hard-on.

     your tumescence.

lend your body
to the night

    the water plunging
    through steel

shall not kneel
or step back

    for your recurring coups.

shit falls on stations
alphabet falls on letters
graffiti falls on planks

on tapes on loops.

when the mind farts
it accumulates in fatal
                    theses

and ripples on paragraphs
                  of water.

there is no present fogged
      no creed fogged
      no fact fogged.

                at its
        shallow side
        where frogs linger,

water goes
        into deep thought.

a drumbeater slides, dives, rolls.

a fishsong for fishmongers
is what is needed
now that stars
are beginning to hide
          in the sky.

about making stories disappear
how is it done?

          put a guffaw on trial.

turn down
          turn down

          overbuyings,
                    dominoes,
          tokens discerned by decks.

stop watching the wave.
          be the wave.
                    the lacing wave.

between basalt cliffs
no one mourns
the loss of statecraft.

a blaze over water
reminds a quayside
that soon the sea
shall round up stoneposts,
tapers and —

should the seafarer
invite tenderness to meander
through returning hairlines

should his fingers
    become racy
        or go idling through
        wingtips of paranoia

—the sea shall watch itself
  riot
      and
  reclaim the storm
      that
  snaps and screams
      and
  whirls past clambacks
  porcupine quills

seeds of clover
flesh of tides.

nobody lives in the city
beside the waters.
only buildings.

and when between
a naked tree and another
a bushranger slackens her pace,

gendered surfing coils
and turns to a spray
dressed in silver

and a painted clay drunk
with secrets and curses
fastens in her feet
mooncalf and basilisk
mushroom and lichen.

nightlong, tea roars
in your tongue

outside it's cold
it's cold outside

the rain is you falling
you dancing higher
        dancing deeper—

fencevaulter,
            troglodyte,

moonman with moontag
        searching for lice
                in night's hair

foraging for roots
in moon-painted lips.

a tumbling crab
in a street of debuting trombones —
that's what you're called.
a waitress trashing an ashcan —
that's what you're called.
trailcrew witch —
                birdcage watcher —
that's what you're called.

incense licks
        your broken typewriter,

        hedges round
                your piano,

sacrilizes your thoughtway.
                your pinkday.

here's to the next time
        rain wets elbows

as your wild breasts sing
making music is
                making love.

when tarot cards get thrown
        they tear at the hide
        of your stained rug

they feed your body
        into a sari
        into a swimsuit

and let it explore
        unlit scabs

this is what hatred
        looks like

what the blending
        of fib and hiatus is

they teach you
        the physics of pain
        the artistry of pleasure

will you ever shriek
the sun
into your bared wetness

or drop from your hook
canecutters' beer cans?

   bomkom! bladyfuul!

but will you? will you?

na wa o! na so life dey!

from illumination to bloodied
epiphany and back:
the route stretches
to aztec sacrifices.

although providence
predicts the final order
will you let a fish tank
desecrate a waterfall?

make you no run o
make you no run.

from a couplet springs
        the cinnamon

from the cinnamon
        a tide flows

popinjays cretins
        float in the tide

a faucet breaks and
        floods its marionettes

over your splintered cot.

were you the one
        who asked for the name

of the town where you
        were pulled out of

bitter hills? water's detritus?
        straw, feather, charred wood?

it's midnight. i'll knit all my parts
mend all my parts
and diaper you —
prise your heart from gathering clouds.

noses,
noses, trumpeting noses

and fingers soaping
          a city,

becoming an event;

          blood jogging
                    across jaws

          into the arms
               of silt;

what else will they not do
          what prank will they
                    not pull;

deftly,
          in haste,
          the rain strides cityward,

air rises
          from
                    curb to curb.

as a stuffed elk waits
ubanwa measures out
the music of milk

dissolves the pauses
the pauses in his reveries
where neons spin
across the opening doors
of his nights

in the urban tangle
his hands play
his feet play
his sounds mount
unscripted symphonies—

casual, wishing, soaring
yet ashore, weaving
sponges, cavities
gliding with the wind
to a grotto of grains

he is no anchorite
seduced by amethysts
nor diadem
enamored of solitude.

if he craves for unrest
if he crossly craves for unrest
unreproved unrest

tell him
he is in all the places
in me he has opened
to choosy bellhops

                        choose on
                        choose on

in all these places
his questions twine
round xylophones
and make my heart slide
to coastal beats

slide on
slide on

for in every way unfathomable
he paints me all over
with kisses

the sea
flees northward
with her arcana.
trouper, what do you
seek in the waterbarn?

the sea's tactile lore
is easy to carry.
what about
her perfidious meddling?

on the run
legs sink on the cheek
of fluvial foam.
a lifeguard
boasts of regulating
drownings.
trouper, what do you
seek in water wars?

the dusk has gone to play pinball.
who will now buy a drink
for a dawn left behind?

graffiti circulates
through sonorous walls.
a house opens.

to gossip and rumor
sketched in oil.
a house opens.

to hammerers.
to slashers.
to slaughter.

assaulted by hailstorms
a seaplane sways
around a seacoast.

i will like to know
why the waterway
abhors padlocks.

at left angles to the anus: currents
at left angles to the anus: refractions
at left angles to the anus: streamings

i will like to know
why the waterwall
moves sideways.

and the breast, child
is the wing you visit
at the pitch of day.

there is this dance
between you and the breast.

for your sake
breezes consent
to reveal their hangovers.

behind me you do not
see a dragonfly come down.
before me you do not
see fishing boats pause midstream.

and you return to the breast again
as hunger reddens your face
reddens your scream

and the bulbed head of a clown
lurks in the insistent sibilance
of your nights—

it bobs, it darts, it nods.

late p.m. downtown
   gothic blather
      parts brick and wet coat

stragglers sort out
      peaches from a heap
         of salmons.

hot foot over hot oil
     beauty singes her flocks —
          boobs, bowheads

            assembling

               ambling.

take yourself
     into your arms.

expel the crocodiles
      under words

that plants grow from.

there the lights are braided.
refrains surround them.
trees listen.

blurry are the scenesters
there.
the scenetunes there.
streets listen.

stony tracks
lie trespassed
and dishevelled —
there are no footprints
to read in them.

reality has not relented there
under a bulldozer's skitter.

running water is shooting out
between scrubbed wards
and sinewed trophies.

i sit in the place
of washstands.
i bisect congruent diagonals.
it's shrink time.
i slip under my tongue.
a waterman
busks for waterstones.

don't just understand.
overstand.
overstand.

the music in a bird
is what you've
broken into two.

slideaway facedown.
your breath is still
besotted with

the eel on a reef.
where you've beached
stars hang on scales
of water.

convey the politics of tides.
unseal the seraglio.
a catafalque's like that.
refusing acclimatization.
at the ankle. where self
climbs the water hill
of self. foaming without
summit. without the ease
to say goodbye to a gunbutt
saying goodnight to a dynastic boater.

at the floor of the lake
lie the semesters.
thieves of climate!
thieves of mollusk!
at the granite's edge
lie the diplomas.
pressured diplomas.
         virulent diplomas.

they break auxiliary
         pencils!
they smash budding
         inkwells!

flayed by scraps
of triadic chords,
tresses of dates,
     radiographies,
     titters,
softest of breaths,
     solace founders.

night is sex
sex is night
i mean the unhelmeted
                        night
of streetcorner traducers —

night is sex.
            the conversation of balding
                                    clocks.

sex is night.
            seeing that ecstasy is not
                            a scribal task.

in glimpses
            bodies magnify
                        night and sex.

the virtualities of.

where's the attic of the sea
forget it. forget it.
flap out and jist
and razz and twist in again

who's the date of the sea
where is he
give me his number
open the eyes
of his toes of his waters

waters smoking waters
waters prodding waters
seeking his eyes and catching
them in alliances of waters

and the words say
we are shy but we are mean
let's kill the letters
before they kill us

midground: all colorists are poets.
the borderguard and the roamer:
are they poets too?

highground: all carvers are salted
poets eyeing dots and tables.
and sweatshirt tailors?

they chorus and clap
and yap about the insurrectionary
tactics of zippering down
and zippering up.

snowmud riddles embarkments.
dawn growls,
uncovers my vanity
and topples it.

my folded legs
wait for a missing scow.

it won't do to submit
to cascades of reveries.

from the mouth of dawn
rolls out the words paradox
is the heretic of all praises.

i cut up lettuce.
        salt potatoes.

cannonades capsize over compost.
            what is
                what is
                    fire's insomnia?

i bathe my son.
            string rattles round his waist.

it won't do solely
            to unweave youth from dusk.

i've seen the swaying nights
the howling doors
of your heart.

i've seen the wandering rains
the bare feet
of your mind.

beside the bed candlelight blinks.
i see a shark's tooth:
your mexican lover's gift to you.

his photograph fringes
the room's shadow.
i see a man loveseeking,
lovebrewing.

bolts on doors
begin to turn
under dreamcaps under breezeways.

what is a switchblade
doing in a flameout?
what an idiotic question!

stretch out the index finger
and grasp the yardstick —
kiss or rust.

not one advice
is taken for granted
from hugbag to lovebag
from dreampearl to dreambin.

riddled with mugging pain
a stonemason's son
inaugurates his black star line

along with arguments
you stuff chocolate into me
and blare your need
for tropical trees
and weather.

motets of yearning are
escaping with winter.
a skymaster in searoad
is escaping in a wet hat.
and making the best
of it all is a shinbone
and a mudbone.

you've roused the piano.
you can't evict it anymore.
when you touch it
and play
it cries.

because the rain
has no shoe
you aim your arrow
at her foot
and hit it once/twice/thrice

ambulant and petulant
you fly into
the dreamrun
of a cloud

bodyeater my hater my biter
do you sleep with astronomy
do you sleep with theology

pills step out of their coats
books cough on a shelf
birds shake their voices
free from the grip of night

do you let your feet
adore the floor just
because the music of
balalaikas are yours, yours

horseshit in a shithouse
the skin of your hatred
brushes up against me
in a theater seat

water unlocks my muscles
but knots the hairs
of my armpit.

a *schwimmeister*
       scuttles around
              a heated pool.

the chained key
       on my wrist
          wags in water.

o turning one
which traces of you
are to be found in me?

          brown cliffs
gleam above me.
my heels hammer
          blue boards.

Other selections in Chris Abani's Black Goat poetry series

GOMER'S SONG poems by Kwame Dawes
72 pages, trade paperback original, $14.95

Gomer's Song is a contemporary reinterpretation of a Bible story. Gomer, a harlot, was the wife of the Old Testament prophet Hosea. But even after marriage to Hosea, she refused to conform to her expected role. In Gomer, poet Dawes finds the subject for a beautiful contemporary exploration on the cost of arriving at freedom with an uneasy grace. This is tender a book with profound lyrical insights.

AUTO MECHANIC'S DAUGHTER
poems by Karen Harryman
84 pages, trade paperback original, $14.95

Charting the vicissitudes of her own life, and the travails and triumphs of the lives of those whom she knows and loves, Harryman's poems travel great distances, both internally and geographically, from the Kentucky of her youth to the California of her present moment (with a detour in Europe). *Auto Mechanic's Daughter* is a lyrical journey into life's private places and the small joys encountered there.

Also Available from Akashic Books

SONG FOR NIGHT by Chris Abani
164 pages, trade paperback original, $12.95

"Chris Abani might be the most courageous writer working right now. There is no subject matter he finds daunting, no challenge he fears. Aside from that, he's stunningly prolific and writes like an angel. If you want to get at the molten heart of contemporary fiction, Abani is the starting point."
—**Dave Eggers,** author of *What Is the What*

"Not since Jerzy Kosinski's *The Painted Bird* or Agota Kristof's Notebook Trilogy has there been such a harrowing novel about what it's like to be a young person in a war. That Chris Abani is able to find humanity, mercy, and even, yes, forgiveness, amid such devastation is something of a miracle."
—**Rebecca Brown,** author of *The End of Youth*

BECOMING ABIGAIL by Chris Abani
A selection of the *Essence Magazine* Book Club and Black Expressions Book Club
128 pages, trade paperback original, $11.95

"Abani is a fiction writer of mature and bounteous gifts . . . Abani, himself incarcerated and tortured for his writings and activism in Nigeria in the mid-'80s, writes about the body's capacity for both ecstasy and pain with an honesty and precision rarely encountered in recent fiction . . ."
—***New York Times Book Review*** (Editors' Choice)